CHOREOGRAPHING SPACE

House Design
HOUSE + HOUSE

CHOREOGRAPHING SPACE

House Design
HOUSE + HOUSE

images
Publishing

5

TEXT BY CATHI & STEVEN HOUSE   INTRODUCTION BY TONY COHAN

First published in Australia in 1999 by
The Images Publishing Group Pty Ltd
ACN 059 734 431
6 Bastow Place, Mulgrave, Victoria 3170, Australia
Telephone +(61 3) 9561 5544 Facsimile +(61 3) 9561 4860
E-mail: books@images.com.au

National Library of Australia Cataloguing-in-Publication Data

House, Steven, 1952–.

House & House choreographing space.

Bibliography.

Includes index.

ISBN 1 86470 029 7.

House Design Series ISSN 1329 0045

1. House, Steven, 1952–. 2. House, Cathi, 1953–.
3. Architects – United States. 4. Architecture, Domestic –
United States – Designs and plans. 5. Architecture, Modern –
20th century – United States – Designs and plans. I. House,
Cathi, 1953–. II. Title. (Series : House design : 5).

728.022273

Designed by The Graphic Image Studio Pty Ltd
Mulgrave, Australia

Printing by Everbest Printing, Hong Kong

CONTENTS

INTRODUCTION

A Few Notes on the Work of House + House by Tony Cohan

'Beauty was the aura surrounding the object, the consequence of the secret relation between its making and its meaning.'
Octavio Paz,
Seeing and Using: Art and Craftsmanship

I first met Cathi and Steven House on a street in San Miguel de Allende, Mexico. At the time they were finishing work on their own house— a remarkable synthesis of Mexican building concepts and artisanship, Mediterranean space and light, and the subtle employment of contemporary ideas. Since then, the house has been much praised, widely featured internationally, and won various design awards.

Even before I saw their house they'd visited mine, an 18th century dwelling in the middle of town with thick adobe walls, soaring interior volumes, and great mesquite doors. I and my artist wife Masako take great pleasure in our house, yet sometimes we'd think of making changes: aligning it more closely to the uses we put it to. When the Houses came to visit, I saw that they immediately grasped its mysteries and paradoxes: what made it sing, what was eccentric or odd about it, and what made us want to change it while keeping it the same. Our old Mexican house and their new one formed the axis of a conversation extending outward into a wide-ranging contemplation of culture and materials, travel and time, life and art. It soon became apparent that the Houses were no ordinary architects.

In his brilliant essay on Mexican art and craftsmanship, the Nobel Prize-winning poet and essayist Octavio Paz says: 'A glass pitcher, a wicker basket, a *huipil* (dress) of coarse cotton cloth, a wooden bowl [are] handsome objects not in spite of but because of their usefulness. Their beauty is inseparable from their function: they are handsome because they are useful. Handicrafts belong to a world existing before the separation of the useful and the beautiful.'

Paz' commentary is not to be constrained by considerations of scale—certainly not in this part of the world, where the hand's touch is equally

Opposite:
Color, composition, light
San Miguel de Allende, Mexico
Photography: Steven House

visible in great monumental architecture, ancient and new: the Mayan, Aztec and Toltec temples, the festive structures one sees in every town and village, the houses and buildings of Luís Barragán. The work of the design firm House + House, grounded equally in the elastic languages of modernism and the world's vernacular architectures, bears the intimate, tactile qualities we associate with the best crafts but wrought larger: evocations of a world before the fragmentation of the industrial age, when use and beauty were inseparable. The Houses understand that, as Leger said: 'Architecture is a natural function. It grows out of the ground, like animals or plants.'

With Steven and Cathi House, architecture does indeed seem like a natural function: they breathe it. Products of a unique, intensive education at Virginia Tech's College of Architecture modeled after the Bauhaus, emphasizing design at all scales and the inter-relatedness of all forms of art and architecture, they began House + House with the full array of practical and theoretical tools at their command. At the same time, a series of extensive, revelatory travels in Asia, the Mediterranean, and Latin America awakened them to the enduring power of indigenous architectures. (One result was their traveling exhibition, 'Mediterranean Indigenous Architecture - timeless solutions for the human habitat,' a critical analysis of village architecture in Greece, Italy, Yugoslavia, and Spain.) Additionally, both draw beautifully; both are exceptional photographers. Cathi House's personal involvement in crafts—sewing, weaving, spinning, painting, working in clay and fabric and plastic, making baskets, rugs, toys, clothes and furniture—lends an added dimension to House + House projects, allowing them to extend their architectural vision down into custom furniture, landscape, and interiors.

This diversity of technical skills, and their ease with genres and eras, gives the design firm of House + House near-infinite range—and the freedom that comes with that. But what really distinguishes its work is the use to which this virtuosity is put: for House + House understands a dwelling as a dialogue among space, materials, and client whose ultimate aim is not to glorify the builder but to illuminate the client's

existence. Far more interested in the 'soul' of a house than its 'look', House + House's conversation with clients more resembles a communion, revolving less around design issues than the quality of experience: What human creative end is trying to be realized? Where do function, esthetics, and pleasure meet? What would release joy? Deeply sensitive to elements of forms, color, texture, natural light, and movement, House + House attempts to create a tangible spirit within each home, molded to the process of living. How will this tree, this slope, this shaft of light be experienced? The result is an intimate, personal architecture, delving to the core of the client's special nature.

Though international in scope, most House + House projects have been built in northern California, within range of their San Francisco office. Contemporary California—eclectic, innovative, multicultural, with an emphasis on the inner life and reaching out for new experience—is a perfect environment for House + House. Such human and geographic diversity requires site-specific, client-specific architecture: projects as unique as those who commission them.

In a world where beauty and function have been sundered, House + House's mission is to knit them back together.

Sometimes when we're in Mexico at the same time, the Houses come over and we sit in the back garden on a stone seat by the old rubble wall, beneath the ring where horses used to tie up, shaded by a jacaranda and a cheremoya tree. We gaze back at the 250-year-old house, decoding its structure, thinking about where things might go without disturbing its soul. We take in the sun's angle, the flow of winds, the migration of light down the walls. We talk about what we saw in the marketplace today, or some fiesta observed, or our recent travels. This rich contemplation of experience is the very wellspring of House + House's architecture, what sets it apart. The Greek architect Aris Konstantinidis, a favorite of theirs, has said: 'Here the landscape comes near us, it comes into the building, not so much because we see it with our eyes, but more because we know it exists, we capture its existence with our senses, we embrace it with our body and soul.'

CHOREOGRAPHING SPACE

by Cathi and Steven House

1

Our journey into awareness began with our travels. After finishing our formal education, we took time to live in Greece. There our lives spun onto a path we could not have imagined. Opening our eyes for the first time on the island of Santorini, we saw the morning sun raking the rough texture of a stucco wall. The power and beauty of it took our breath away and solidified our concept of architecture. Since then we have looked to our travels as a source of inspiration and personal growth. It is during those times that we are renewed in our work, our visions, our selves, and are able to let go of preconceptions, see the world with open eyes, and explore new ways of thinking. In one of those special moments that can change you forever, we happened into the open door off the roof of a little chapel. In that tiny space we discovered a stair that amazed and delighted us. So unique was the design that it taught us we must question everything, never make assumptions, and that we must always search beyond our imagination. To create magic—

to amaze and delight our clients and give them breathless moments—is a goal that has guided our firm's work for the past 16 years.

Wandering village paths revealed to us how space can be choreographed. The excitement and anticipation is overwhelming as you turn this way and that, always aware that something new is about to unfold. The path widens, the wall becomes a seat, you move like a dancer up meandering stairs, through a colonnade, around a fountain... We learned to see not just with our eyes but with our souls. As we shape buildings, we often talk of choreographing space, composing and relating spaces and materials to enhance the journeys through the daily rituals that each home contains. We think of movement—spiritually, visually, emotionally, as well as physically—and search for the same quality of experience in the trip from the bedroom to the kitchen as one finds in a stroll through a little Italian village. The journey must address each aspect differently to achieve that magic and mystery.

Color, texture and light are powerful tools in shaping the environment. Studying patterns in old stone walls, the shimmer of morning light or layered tones of colored washes, has taught us that color, texture and light are inextricably intertwined. How we use them differs with each project. Sometimes it is a search for unity, a link to nature, a reference to history— to sculpt form, to focus a view, to invite passage. We may use them to define space, enrich a material or highlight a detail. We often blend color with light to create a mood by casting a wash of color or a shimmering glow. Understanding color begins with the site— the rocks, branches, bark, leaves, grasses, lichen, moss and soil. They change from sunrise to sunset and with the seasons. Selecting building materials is a search for the palette that will complement the land and embrace the clients and their possessions. We celebrate each material and work closely with the craftsmen who form them.

We look for moments of pause in the homes we create, those spaces that are not programmed— the surprises—and in each home they are different. That moment when you are between spaces, between thoughts, between activities— in which you can take a breath, remove your coat, change your mind—is incredibly powerful. We never know where they will surface, but we are always searching for their potential development.

When we are designing, we imagine how our clients will feel as they move through their lives within their home. Composition, proportion, movement, focus, vistas, color, textures, light, touch, reflection, pause, glimpse, surprise, wonder, joy—these are some of our tools. We take great pleasure in discovering how to use them in new ways with each client to create homes which embrace and celebrate their lives.

2

3

1   Batik - Stairs in Mykonos, Greece
2   Movement - Chechaouen, Morocco
3   Texture - Atlas Mountains, Morocco
4   Composition - Miranda, Italy
5   Sketch analysis of progression - Assisi, Italy
Images: Steven House (2,4,5); Cathi House (1,3)

4

'Architecture...is not only buildings, but all the works that man makes with his hands in the course of his daily occupations.'

HEIDEGGER

'...it will be better, not for the streets to run straight, but to have them wind about like the course of a river. Besides appearing so much longer, they will conduce very much to beauty and convenience. Moreover, this winding of the streets will make the passenger at every step discover a new structure, and...in the winding of the streets there will be no house but what, in some part of the day, will enjoy some sun; nor will they be without gentle breezes; and yet they will not be molested by stormy blasts, because such will be broken by the turning of the streets.'

ALBERTI

'When one has completed the necessary one comes immediately upon the beautiful and pleasant.'

VOLTAIRE

'The ideal house is one that does not contain anything superfluous and that lacks nothing necessary.'

PLUTARCH

'The true work of architecture is not a monument but a receptacle of life.'

ARIS KONSTANTINIDIS

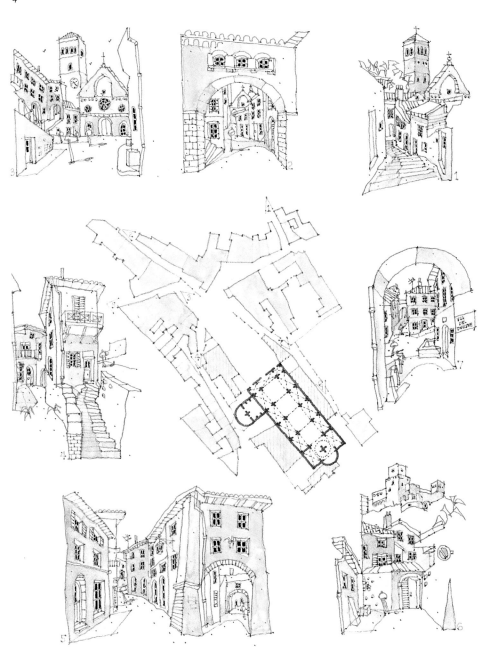

5

TELEGRAPH HILL RESIDENCE

San Francisco, California, USA
Design/Completion 1992/1994

1

A tiny 1906 earthquake relief home nestled at the end of a narrow alley on Telegraph Hill had been remodeled in the 1930s and expanded in the 1950s. The home had an awkward plan, low ceilings, dark spaces and an array of odd materials. Positioned in the center of the block, this is a distinctly urban setting, yet is surrounded by its neighbor's gardens. Directly behind the home stood a large Japanese maple tree. Preservation of this beautiful tree became a focal point for the new design.

The addition was demolished, the remaining structure gutted and 400 square feet added. It is still a tiny bungalow from the street that gives no clue to the surprise contained within. Carefully skewed geometry allowed the tree to be incorporated into the center of the home, framed by a soaring grid of windows. A curving stairway wraps the bar, defining the kitchen and connecting to an open bridge flying above to the master bedroom. Cabinets are dyed purple, continuing the color of the carpet. Black knobs, appliances, sink and laminate counters complete a composition which begins with the black hex-crete concrete bar counter. Swirls ground into the aluminum facing sparkle at the foot of the stair. An arc of perforated steel at the master bedroom deck recalls the forms inside, screening for privacy while filtering sunlight. Radiating lines scored into the rose colored concrete further accentuate the rigorous geometry. Sculpted walls shape the space and form niches, each washed with light from geometric fixtures and carefully aligned skylights. A rhythmic procession of steel angles and cables is capped with turquoise stained maple railing at the flying bridge above.

The living room opens onto a spacious deck connected to the garden below where old, stone paving, lemon trees, and foundations of an old church recall the site's history. Smooth plywood siding stained gray and turquoise provides crisp form on the exterior, at once in scale with the neighborhood, while denying scale altogether.

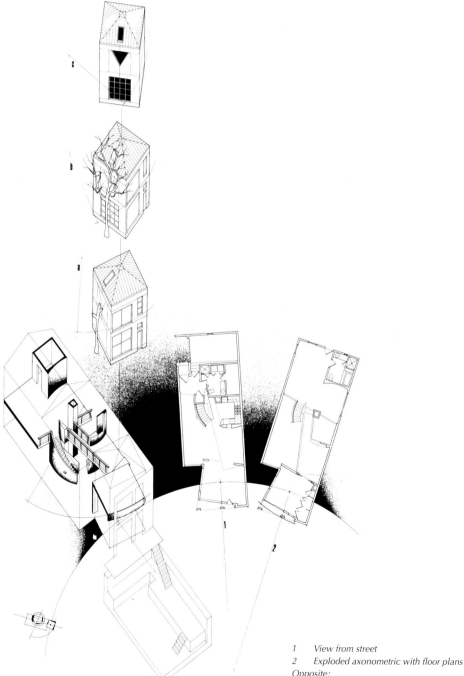

1   View from street
2   Exploded axonometric with floor plans
Opposite:
      Rear facade from garden

2

4

6

7

8

5

4   View to stair with bridge above
5   Kitchen
6   View to living room from second floor
7   Master bathroom
8   Detail of stair at bar
Opposite:
    View of living area from entry

JARVIS RESIDENCE

Oakland, California, USA
Design/Completion 1995/1997

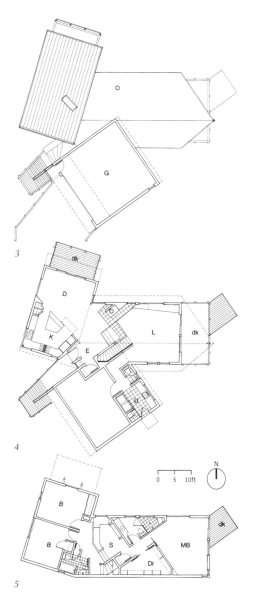

1

This site, a steep, north facing hillside on a quiet cul-de-sac, was among those left bare by Oakland's tragic firestorm. Three intersecting volumes layer down the site with the garage at the top, living spaces in the middle and private spaces below. Complex massing orients each level to its views. The entry winds down an exterior stairway to a front porch with a sand-blasted glass door under a galvanized steel canopy. The kitchen and dining room bask in the afternoon sun and enjoy the twinkling evening lights of San Francisco. Under the living room's butterfly ceiling, views are focused onto a spacious deck and quiet canyon beyond. Two bedrooms and a study share the lower floor with the master bedroom which opens onto its own private deck and garden.

Long vistas through layered space unfold inside. The forms are strong and deliberate, yet this is a warm and comfortable home, made for living. The plan is open with divisions created by shape and object, while each space feels clearly defined. There is a chaotic quality in the angular intersections and the sloping ceilings, yet the spaces evoke a Zen-like serenity.

Careful placement of windows and skylights bring a glow into each volume at different times of the day. By capturing the rising cool air from the canyon below, the house is naturally ventilated. The living spaces are anchored together by the fireplace. A composition of rough stucco, polished stainless steel and the tenuous balance of the maple wedge create an inner focal point. Butt glazed windows allow portions of the walls to disappear. Inside, bird's-eye maple cabinets and flooring, African slate, concrete counters and stainless steel feel warm and natural. Outside, galvanized steel light fixtures, canopies and railings reflect the colors of their surroundings. Stucco, integrally colored in soft earth tones, borrows from the hues of trees and grasses, harmoniously tying the complex, opposing forms with the land.

2

3

4

5

1   West facade from street
2   East facade
3   Garage floor plan
4   Upper floor plan
5   Lower floor plan
Opposite:
    Detail of canopy at garage door

8

9

Opposite:
    View of dining room and kitchen
8   View of dining room and fireplace
    from living room
9   Kitchen
10 Master bathroom

10

LANGMAID RESIDENCE

Oakland, California, USA
Design/Completion 1992/1994

Without warning a tragic firestorm in 1991 took the home these clients had lived in for 20 years. They had loved their home; loss and necessity brought them to us. They came wanting their home back.

The original home, built in 1911, was a simple two-story box with formal living spaces at the front, kitchen and utility spaces in the back, bedrooms upstairs. Set back on the site with a large front yard, it had no privacy from the long street frontage. Analysis of the old house and detailed diagrams of the potential the site offered helped our clients realize that there was no reason to recreate their old home.

The deeper we inquired into what they had actually loved about the home, the more we all realized that it was their memories and the quality of light in the dining room. The house was gone; the light was still there. As we discussed private rituals and analyzed their life, a layout emerged which thrust the main living spaces toward the street from which they had so retreated in the former home. The configuration tested their new understanding. The process of discovery became a process for learning and healing for them.

Continued...

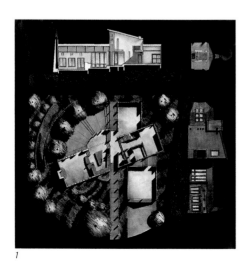

1   Site/floor plan with
    section and elevation
2   View from private
    terrace

house
+house

Graphic Design
stre

Steve ..... AIA
..athi..
..99 .....to
San ....ornia
Telephone ... 474 2112

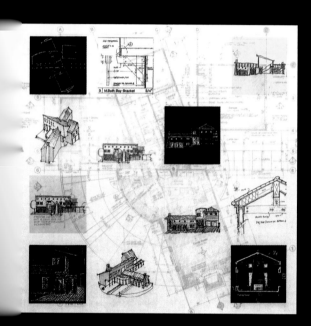

THE ... OF 1991

4

Opposite:
Concept design studies
4   *Front facade from street*
5   *View of private terrace from living room*

This 4,000-square-foot home is designed with an axial geometry of two intersecting wings. The family/kitchen/dining wing divides the front yard into public and private gardens. The open plan is linked by a sweeping curve which shapes the floor-to-ceiling windows of the eating area and the built-in audiovisual cabinet dividing the family and kitchen areas. Spacious terraces and careful garden planning provide strong indoor-outdoor relationships and focus to views previously ignored. The light they had loved in their old dining room now pours into every room through shaped windows.

A trellised arcade leads to the front door, sand-blasted in a pattern describing geometric concepts in the home. A burgundy column stands at the centerpoint of the intersecting forms. The canted newel post of the gridded oak railing anchors the stairway to the bedrooms above. Lofty ceilings and carefully placed windows and skylights in the upper gallery invite patterns of light that change throughout the day. Protruding bays at the bedrooms create window seats, a study alcove, and details on the exterior to articulate the building mass. The curve of the eating area below provides a private deck and deep sitting area for the master bedroom. Details in wood, stucco and copper respect the history and traditional atmosphere of the neighborhood, which included excellent examples of Craftsman and Mission Revival style houses from the early 1900s.

Vertical grain oak cabinetry, exposed Douglas fir trusses, and exterior cedar siding are stained translucent turquoise to complement copper-plated steel brackets and copper inlays in the floor. Colored concrete terraces and counters reflect the coppery clay tile roofing. The stucco flows inside as steel troweled plaster on the fireplace wall and the colors continue in soft handwashes on the walls and ceilings. A fading pattern of sand-blasting at the windows flanking the fireplace provides privacy from the sidewalk and street, with clear views to the sky and treetops beyond.

5

7

8

9

Opposite:
   View of kitchen, dining and family
   areas
7   *View of family room toward kitchen*
8   *View of dining room toward stair*
9   *View of kitchen from dining room*

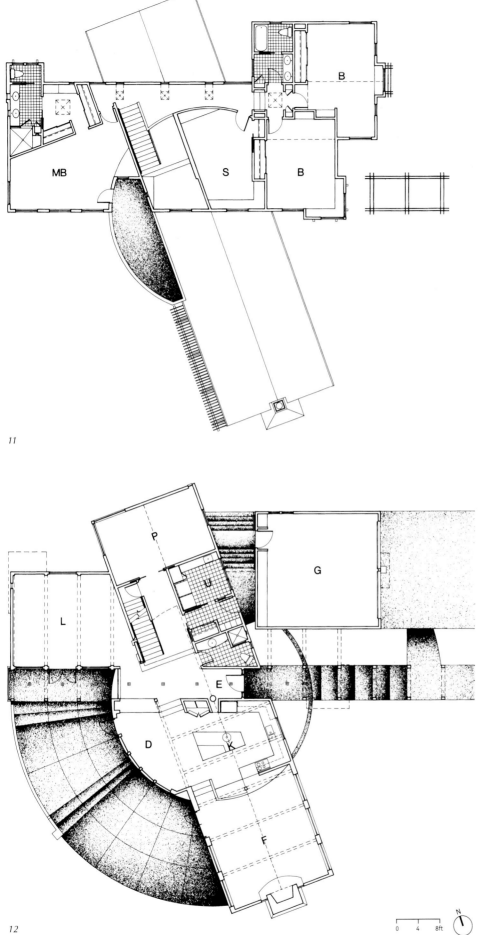

11

12

13

14

15

Opposite:
  Family room and fireplace
11 Second floor plan
12 First floor plan
13 Master bathroom
14 Children's bathroom vanity
15 Powder bathroom vanity

17

18

19

20

WALDHAUER RESIDENCE

Woodside, California, USA
Design/Completion 1989/1991

Energy conservation, thoughtful use of natural resources and poetic harmony with the land were the guiding requirements for this home for an inventor/musician and an environmental scientist. Their site is a windswept hillside of golden California grasses and treacherous cliffs on the Pacific coast with panoramic views over canyons and wooded hills. A grove of oak trees, a protected meadow, and a large boulder marked with ancient Indian grinding have been preserved. The building form derives from a geometric framework inspired by site characteristics. The roof slope follows the topography, deflecting occasional gale force winds. The curving wing provides a wind-break for a protected entry garden. Alignments acknowledge sunset at the winter solstice when the family gathers. Solar orientation takes advantage of heat gain in winter, with a deep trellis on the west providing protection from summer sun. Convection pulls cool air from the canyon below up through low windows and out clerestory windows, providing natural cooling and ventilation.

The main living spaces are contained within a single volume, bound by two powerful walls shaped by the land. Guest bedrooms and utility spaces occupy a simple container. The garage roof marks the top of the ridge. A tower acts as a fulcrum holding the pieces together. Interstitial spaces are accidental, like the spaces between the trees. The skewed master bedroom and tower align with sunset over the most prominent mountain peak. An open plan choreographs a sequence of revealed and concealed glimpses of the landscape. Softly stained redwood siding blends with the soil and stones indigenous to this site. The wood floor evokes the soft golden hues of the native grasses. Plastered in mottled shades of green, the tower reflects the moss and lichen covered trees.

1   East facade from street
2   South facade
3   Exploded axonometric view
Opposite:
    West facade

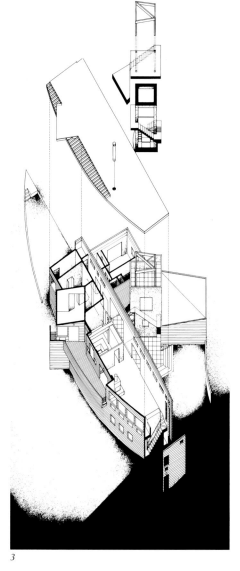

6

7

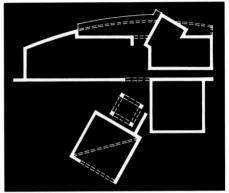

8

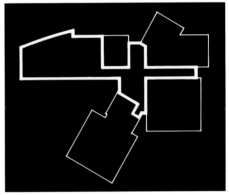

9

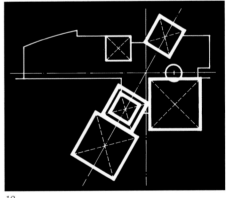

10

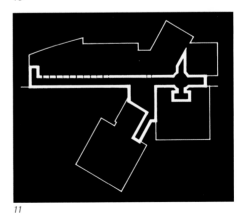

11

PRIVATE RESIDENCE

Hillsborough, California, USA
Design/Completion 1986/1988

In an affluent community south of San Francisco, this 9,600-square-foot house draws on the traditional architecture of its neighbors yet stands on its own as a modern villa. The corner site was originally the front yard of one of Hillsborough's original and most beautiful mansions. This new house was oriented to play against the stately home across the street. Facing a quiet cul-de-sac, its four-car-garage is around the corner, buried in a grove of mature trees offering protection from any street sounds and eliminating garage doors from the front facade. The form draws its proportions and stylistic references from northern Italian villas, yet this is a California home with a focus on indoor-outdoor living and the needs of a family who entertain often on a large scale.

Two concepts are interwoven throughout this home. The first, dealing with layout and organization, includes symmetry, axiality, progression and layering of space. The primary axis from the circular drive to the pool terrace is intersected by an 85-foot-long circulation gallery. Floor-to-ceiling windows at each end of the gallery focus on two magnificent trees. A vertical axis at the intersection evokes a tie to heaven as

Continued...

1   Section at living room
2   Rear facade from pool

3

3   Front facade from street
4   Conceptual design sketch
Opposite:
    View of rear terrace

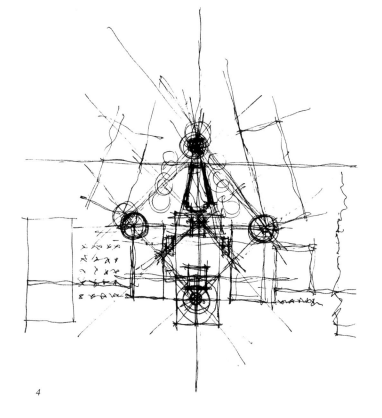

4

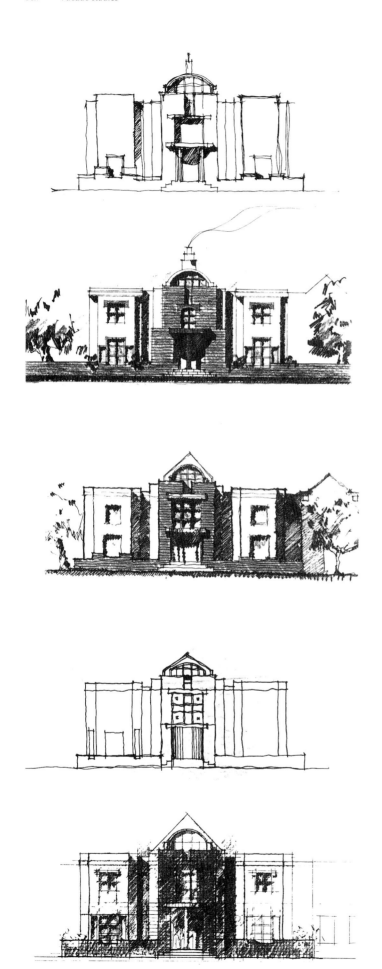

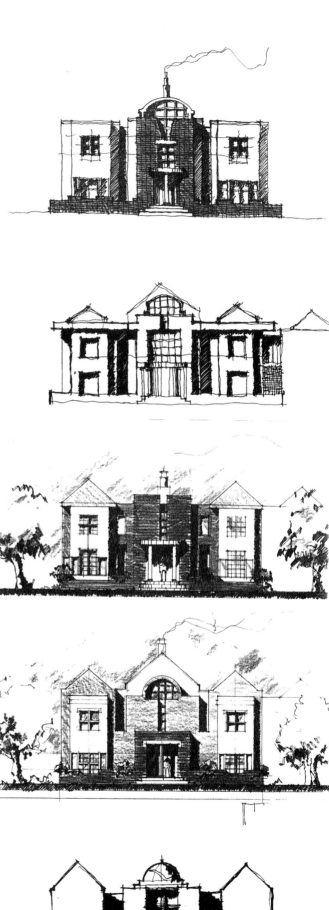

6

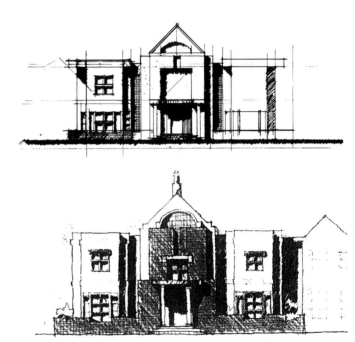

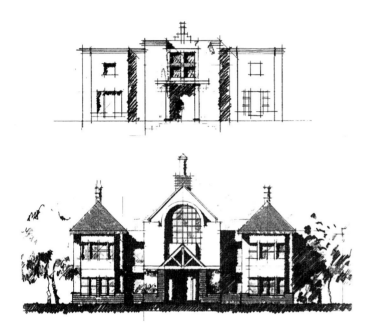

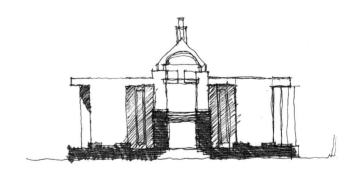

7

a shaft of light penetrates a deep vertical skylight and a glass block 'window' in the second floor. Progression within the house leads through layer after layer of composed facades with vistas to and beyond each space. It is a formal house with formal divisions of space, with primary and secondary circulation, symmetrical in the overall plan and within the rooms. The living spaces spill out onto sun-drenched terraces, a pool, spa, and to gardens enclosed by stands of mature trees.

The second concept guides the detailing and use of materials to achieve more than the budget would allow. Simple construction afforded the use of some finer materials. Double framed walls provide a sense of solidity, strength and permanence appropriate to a home of this scale and historic reference. The play of light and shadows on the thick walls is further enhanced by simple shaping, soffiting, articulation and varying ceiling heights. French limestone flooring

and blocks are shaped into details at the fireplace, handrail and wedge-shaped art pedestals. Stone columns are hand-cut in Italy to exact proportions dictated by Vitruvius. The entry is capped with a copper pyramid and the front door and railings reflect the stepped details and forms of the house. The interior walls are hand-painted and the stucco is hand-rubbed to the luster of the limestone.

8

9

10

11

12

8   Composite rendering
9   View of living room from entry
10 Detail at balcony railing
11 View toward entry from living room
12 Detail at gallery niche

14

15

16

17

GRANDVIEW ESTATE

Oakland, California, USA
Design/Completion 1993/1996

1

When the 1991 Oakland firestorm struck, we were in the process of remodeling a home for our clients. Gone with those flames were the old home's limitations and everything our clients owned. From the ashes came the opportunity for something new, and the chance for us to help them rebuild their lives. A new site helped our clients disconnect from the past and embrace the future.

This 4,000-square-foot home is a celebration of family and life. To incorporate our client's strong spiritual ideals it was necessary to delve deeply into their hearts. They wanted to incorporate ideas from feng shui and geomancy, concepts we had worked with previously. While analyzing sun angles, we noted solar alignments on significant days in their lives. While studying the views and vegetation, we also traced energy flows and spiritually powerful zones within the site. As we began to layout the rooms and relate them to each other, we aligned them with sunsets on specific days and set angles related to spiritual energies.

The result is a home with meaning in every move. The sweep of the entry wall with its deep-set windows embraces the home, protecting it from the intrusions of the street. The curve continues in a carefully proportioned wave through the home, setting up key elements that define the interior spaces. An arc in the ceiling marks the invisible edge of the dining room. The sensual, snaking, free-standing kitchen cabinets split apart to offer glimpses of views and precious spots for new objects. The circular stair follows a natural energy flow, tying the family centers together.

Continued...

2

1   View from street
2   Detail of steel posts at master balcony
Opposite:
    Detail of openings at front wall

4

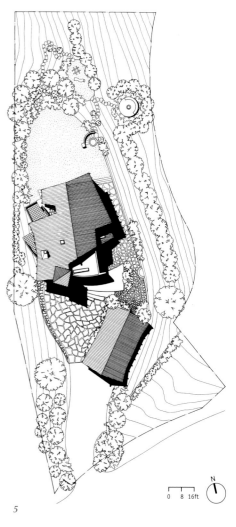

5

6

7

8

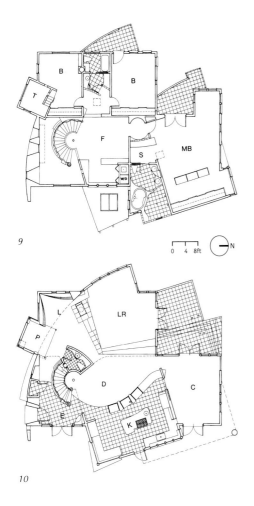

9

0 4 8ft (N)

10

4   Front wall at entry
5   Site plan
6   Copper sconce detail
7   Detail at wall
8   Detail at splayed window
9   Second floor plan
10 First floor plan
11 Master bathroom
12 Kitchen

12

11

The body of the home finds its orientation in alignments to the husband's birthday; the angle of the kitchen and master bath celebrates the wife's sensual, nurturing nature and embraces the sunrise on her birthday; the master bed is aligned with sunset on their anniversary. Colors dance and play, celebrating their joys.

Colors are layered upon each other to define the forms and draw the eye. Materials are detailed to question normal assumptions. Steel curves and curls, glass waves, stone floats, and wood in unusual tones, feels natural. The marble kitchen counters contrast the hand-blown glass light fixtures and complement the multi-colored

cabinets and hand-painted accent walls. In the master bath shaped layers of peach limestone float over lavender and celadon tinted cabinets matched to the green hues of glass sinks and tiles and lavender steel troweled plaster. Wood is finished in luminous, pearlized tones; steel is hand-molded into embracing forms; glass is hand-blown to glisten with light and color. Each material celebrates its nature and the highly skilled hands of the artisans who formed and finished it.

13

14

13   Stair at entry
14   Detail of cabinets from dining room
15   Detail of shelving at library

15

GRANDVIEW

16

17

18

19

20

BUCKINGHAM WAY RESIDENCE

Hillsborough, California, USA
Design/Completion 1990/1992

When a commercial photographer with contemporary taste chose for his family to live in a community of traditional homes, they decided to hide their private lives inside a nondescript suburban ranch house.

As the first phase of a total house renovation, this 1,000-square-foot kitchen/family room remodel transforms the uninspired tract interior into a space of soaring volumes, natural light and sensuous materials. The design solution began with complete demolition of the kitchen cabinets, appliances, windows, doors, flooring, interior finishes, fireplace surround, and the ceiling to reclaim the volumes lost in the attic.

Removal and restructuring of the wall between the kitchen and family area further opened the rooms, creating the illusion of more space. The kitchen cabinets were reshaped and thrust through a new glass wall while a shaped and skewed free-standing partition creates new definitions of space and separation between the family room and informal dining area. The owner's hand is felt in the design of the dining table, a lamp, and in the finishes of the steel column.

Newly defined volumes and a complex geometry of angled lines and planes are integrated into a palette of natural, monochromatic materials. Bird's-eye maple cabinets are dyed silver gray; the stainless steel appliances and backsplash shimmer against reflective black granite counters; a black slate floor is the backdrop to natural steel troweled plaster burnished to mottled shades. Steel pipe columns are finished in three textures to emphasize the new forms as they define the thrust of the kitchen window and locate the center of the geometric spiral that shapes the cabinets. The conical steel bar sink with etched glass counter and curving wall creates a focal point for both the family room and the entry. Glass block walls add depth to the entry and sparkle with sunlight from new skylights.

1

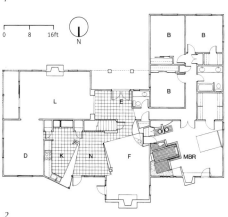

0   8   16ft   N

2

1   View of kitchen window from terrace
2   New foor plan
Opposite:
    View of nook from kitchen

Opposite:
View of kitchen
5 *Detail of dividing wall*
6 *Exploded axonometric
   view*

5

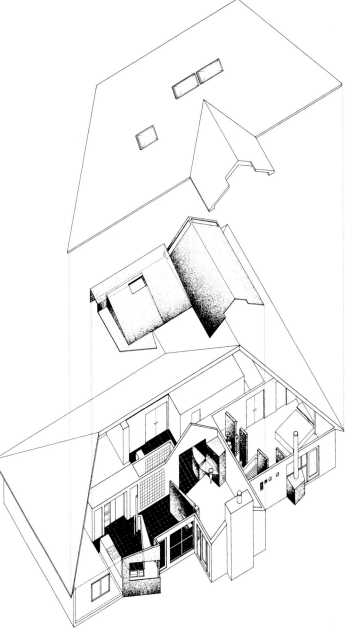

6

7   Fireplace at family room
8   Detail at cooktop
9   Detail of slit in wall
10 Detail at steel column in kitchen

7

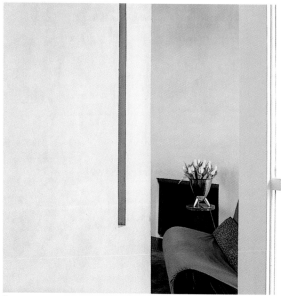

8

9

THE HOMESTEAD

Nevada City, California, USA
Design/Completion 1991/1994

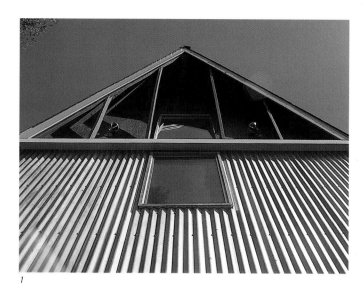

1

An exhaustive search for contractors introduced us to one who did not have the experience yet had an attention to detail that convinced us to give him a chance. Our relationship was tumultuous at first. We learned, argued and listened to each other and over time mutual respect grew. After our sixth home together he said he would not build another, unless the next was his!

He and his wife purchased a secluded wooded lot in the Sierra Nevada foothills. All of the imagery they had collected pointed to an old country farmhouse. We decided that we would create one, something new but with a history of its own.

We created a fictional story about a compound of rural buildings connected over the years into a rambling 3,500-square-foot house. The family, kitchen and breakfast areas, with the master suite above, form the 'original house proper'. The high ceilinged living room and stair are the 'barn' with additional bedrooms, office and laundry as an 'addition'. The garage and dining room are 'sheds' that link and complete the farmhouse which appears to have grown over the years.

The triangular site added to the story, offering interesting opportunities in the form of the home. We detailed the 'house proper' with painted, shiplap wood siding and traditionally trimmed windows. The 'barn' is finished in broad rough sawn boards with transparent stain, the 'sheds' in smaller rough sawn boards. The wrap-around-porch is partly enclosed to become the informal dining area, detailed to look 'remodeled', with the 'old' porch ceiling carrying through. The dining room 'shed' is an infill piece, resolving the geometries of intersecting

Continued...

1   Window detail
2   Detail of canted gabled roof
Opposite:
    Front facade from street

2

4

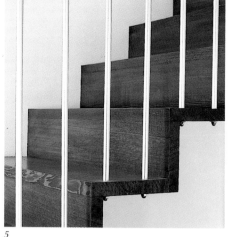

5

pieces. Another 'shed' over the garage and laundry area completes the compound. Two chimney towers in corrugated galvanized steel and alternating wood siding flank the entry.

Heavy wood beams trim the large living room window and the stepped ribbon of wood stairs is hung with delicate aluminum tubes.

Colors are drawn directly from the surrounding vegetation. Burgundy manzanita bark leads to the red front door, the canted gabled roof and the deep wine color of the wood floor. Shades of blue and green lichen on the oaks outside the kitchen window inspired a soft, translucent wash on the cabinetry. The soft gray/green wood siding complements the underside of leaves while the strong trim colors match the tops.

6

7

8

9

10

FOREST VIEW RESIDENCE

Hillsborough, California, USA
Design/Completion 1989/1992

When these clients first called us they were knowledgeable about architecture, wanted something bold and original, had a collection of Corbusier and Macintosh furniture, and had admired our work. They had four children during the 10 years they had lived in their home in an affluent community south of San Francisco, and needed to double its size to 5,400 square feet. Excited by their call, and anxious to meet them, we hesitated on arrival, convinced that we must have the wrong address. What we encountered was a nondescript, 50-year-old Tudor revival house.

Given their traditional attitude the local design review board would probably not approve what our clients wanted. We therefore decided to use the existing home as a front. Our greatest inspiration came from the existing footprint. Most of the new space was added to the south side of the L-shaped home, creating a large sunny courtyard with a small second floor addition at the rear. The angle of the side yard set the geometries in motion. The addition is composed of a series of archetypal building forms: cylinder, cube, wedge, cone. New walls are formed along abstract lines such as swinging arcs and piercing planes. Other spaces are shaped by

Continued...

1   Fountain at entry
2   Rear facade

property lines, setbacks and existing foundations. Rhythms of windows and columns add order; spaces flow into and through each other, open, yet divided by shape, ceilings and materials.

A long wedge-shaped addition easily housed the new living and dining rooms. The existing home was gutted and reorganized to provide the numerous bedrooms, baths and play spaces necessary for a family of six. The old living room was demolished and new kitchen and family rooms were built, reoriented to the rear yard with terraces spilling down to a pool, spa, barbecue, poolhouse and grassy play areas. The master suite was located at the second floor for privacy.

Landscaping screens the existing home from the street and a new ceremonial entry gate pulls focus to a side yard entry garden with a fountain and lavender grasses. The courtyard, an outdoor room within the house becomes the center of all activities. A two-story curving wall at the end of the courtyard is focused from the courtyard fountain, from which radiate lines that define the vaulted stair tower thrusting through a two-story glass wall at the rear facade. The warped plane of the living room roof directs sunlight into the courtyard and the ring of windows in the circular breakfast area captures light from sunrise to sunset. The master bedroom is accessible and open but can be isolated by a series of folding doors. Purple neon in the master shower enriches the lavender plaster walls. The home is filled with windows that capture vistas of the sky and treetops, very calculatedly placed to avoid seeing adjacent homes.

Integrally colored stucco in shades of rose and lavender articulate the various wall surfaces. Cantera stone floors are chiseled smooth inside and rough hewn in the courtyard. Woodwork throughout is Douglas fir, stained a semi-transparent turquoise. Black granite counters seem to disappear, curving, copper-plated steel fireplace shields seem to float and surround sound above the master shower provides an unforgettable bathing experience.

4

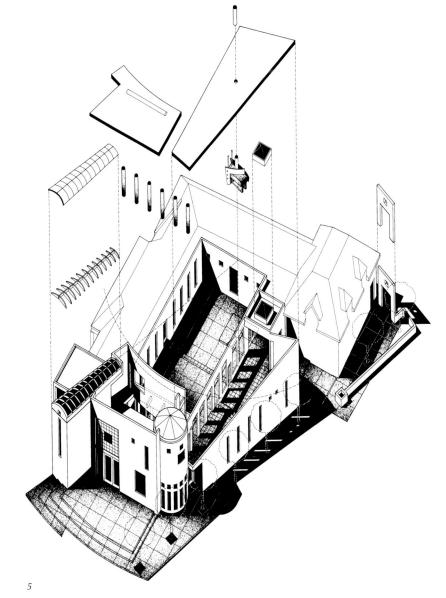

Opposite:
   Dining room
4   *Living room with dining room beyond*
5   *Exploded axonometric view*

5

6

7

8

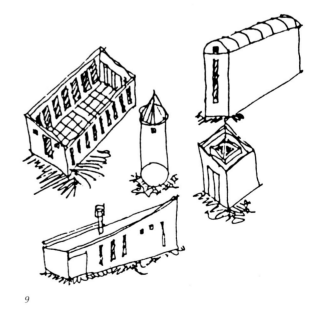

9

6 Courtyard
7 View of master bedroom and stair railing
8 Counter at family room
9 Concept form studies

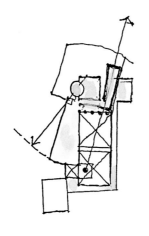

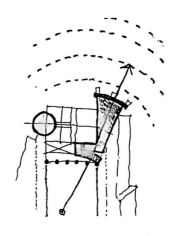

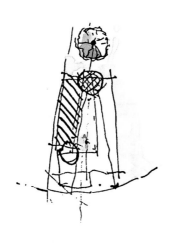

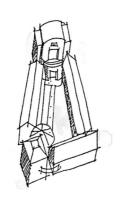

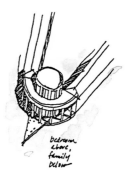

bedroom
above,
family
below

10

11

12

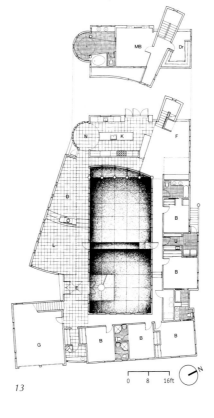

13

10   Concept sketches
11   Kitchen
12   View from stair landing
13   Second floor and new first floor plan

0   8   16ft

14   *Master shower*
15   *Detail at kitchen island*
16   *Detail at fireplace*
17   *View of courtyard columns from family room*
Opposite:
   Master bedroom

14

15

16

17

STINE
RESIDENCE

La Honda, California, USA
Design/Completion 1989/1991 & 1996/1997

1

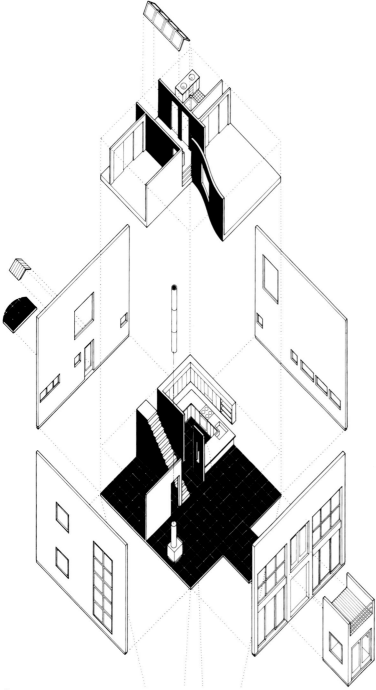

2

The San Francisco Bay Area is one of the most expensive in the United States to build a home. This has presented us with a challenge that we take seriously in each of our projects, but none more seriously than with this home. A young couple walked into our office one day, introducing themselves as neighbors. They wanted us to know how much they had enjoyed looking at the models in our window and had fantasized about having us design a home for them. The cost of the site they had purchased about an hour south of San Francisco had taken most of their funds, leaving them very little with which to build a home.

To build a home within their budget would require careful choices of materials and methods of construction. We decided that a simple, box-like form, built with standard materials doing double duty where possible, might give us the opportunities this home needed. No labor could be afforded cutting or finishing anything special.

A square plan contains all of the living spaces and a guest/study at the lower floor, with two bedrooms, bath and a double high ceiling over the living at the second floor. A small extension provides a music studio at the lower level and a terrace off the master above. Using plywood sheathing to resist earthquakes and, to avoid labor costs in cutting, the house dimensions are set to seven sheets of plywood wide by two sheets high. To eliminate the cost of siding over the plywood, a cedar ply was added and became the finished exterior surface.

Continued...

1   View from below
2   Exploded axonometric view
Opposite:
    East facade

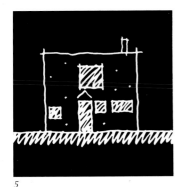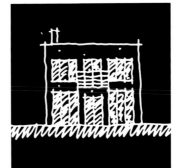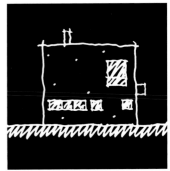

5

6

Slab-on-grade concrete was the most economical foundation, and was colored and scored to produce a beautiful finished floor. Inexpensive, stock aluminum windows are mulled together to create huge expanses of glass looking out into the redwoods or individual units are composed within the facades to relate the rooms to the site. Radiant heating supplements the home's passive solar orientation providing comfort cost effectively. Black laminate counters, birch plywood cabinets, and color on the curving wall complete a simple palette of materials.

Four years later our clients asked if it was possible to double the size of their home to accommodate their growing family—at the same budget. A new master suite, two more bedrooms, a family room and a new entry were added. To make the home relatively maintenance free the entire building, including a new gabled roof, was wrapped in corrugated, galvanized steel.

This simple, 3,000-square-foot home, is nestled in the California coastal hills for a very modest budget. With its new siding the house sometimes glistens and sometimes disappears into the trees, reflecting the colors around it.

Opposite:
  West facade from hill
5   *Elevation studies*
6   *View from front yard*

7

8

9

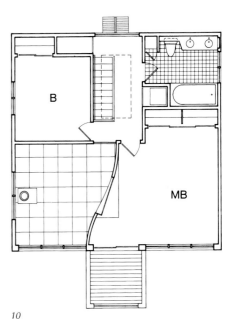

10

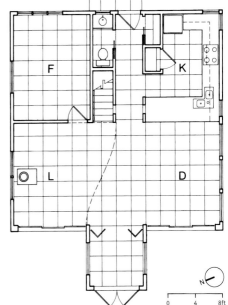

11

7 Living room
8 Detail at high windows
9 View of dining and kitchen areas from living room
10 Second floor plan
11 First floor plan

Opposite:
Balcony detail with new siding
13 *New facade from front yard*
14 *Detail at plant wires*
15 *South facade detail*

13

14

15

A HOUSE FOR
TWO ARCHITECTS

San Miguel de Allende, Mexico
Design/Completion 1994/1996

We have always looked to our travels as one of our greatest sources of inspiration and personal growth—for it is there that we are renewed in our work, our visions, ourselves. It was during one of those travels in Mexico that we stumbled upon a little ruin which captured our hearts and ignited our fantasy about having a retreat in an exotic, far-away land.

We discovered San Miguel de Allende quite by chance 10 years ago while searching for the source of a stone that we use often. San Miguel, in Mexico's Central Highlands, is a 450-year-old Spanish colonial town, protected as a National Historic Monument since the turn of the century. Rich in cultural heritage and modern amenities, it is full of ancient churches, cobblestone streets and crumbling stone walls draped in bougainvillea. On one hand San Miguel is a vision of Mexico at its best, frozen in time, alive, with its ancient cultures and traditions almost untouched by the changes around them. On the other, it has become a center for the arts and contemporary culture.

All indications were that it would probably be a nightmare to build in Mexico. Working in another country, another language, understanding foreign customs has its challenges. As we developed our design and met builders, we discovered the world of artisans and craftsmen who abound there. We decided to celebrate every material, process, and hand that touched any part of our home. We used only local materials and details and decided that our home would be made without power tools.

The rooms and courtyard, stairways, balconies and roof terraces—all interweave into a complex little village. The journeys between the spaces and the vistas to and through them give form and a sense of dimension that belie the truth.

Continued...

1   Front facade from street
2   Front door detail
Opposite:
    Courtyard with kitchen and outdoor dining area

At the lower level the main living spaces open onto and flow through the central courtyard. Guest quarters and an architecture studio find separation and privacy on the second floor.

We began with a beautiful old door that led to remnants of crumbling buildings on a piece of land only 37 feet x 52 feet. Our property is the last piece of an old hacienda that had been divided among children and grandchildren over the years, until all that was left was the front door. Only five blocks from the center of town, this is a dense urban setting where homes touch each other, holding wide to their property lines and opening to a central courtyard. Out of respect for the history of the site, everything that was existing was kept in one form or another.

The entry door was preserved intact and the adobe street wall was reinforced to carry the new roof and second floor, expressing its thickness in the art ledge in the living room. The footprint of the original outhouse is incorporated into the new master bath while a storage shed became one of the studios. Existing stone paving was recut and reused, and brick floors in the living room and studio are as they were. All of the plants that lived there, live there still, but for a peach tree that lives on in the garden of one of the workers.

The roof tiles were reclaimed from collapsed buildings. The brick railings and boveda ceiling are specialties of the region. Railings, hinges, hardware and furniture were forged in fire and

Continued...

6

5

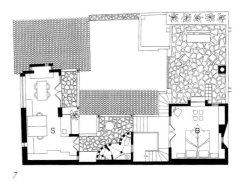

7

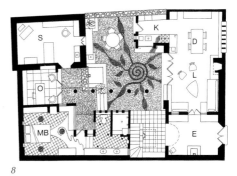

8

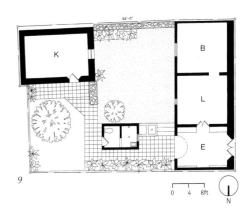

9

0   4   8ft

N

Opposite:
  View of stair from entry
5 *Stairway*
6 *Courtyard paving detail*
7 *New second floor plan*
8 *New first floor plan*
9 *Original site and first floor plan*

10

11

12

10 View of dining room from living room
11 View of dining room from kitchen
12 View of kitchen from dining room

13

14

15

16

hammered into shape from raw steel. Black slate from nearby mountains is broken and set on edge in the courtyard paving, combined with ochre colored stones, hand collected from a dry river bed just outside of town, all in a pattern that tells part of the story of our lives. Black Cantera stone is hand-cut into columns, rain and fountain spouts, and faces the tall living room wall. The kitchen is positioned and open shelves designed to showcase the existing stone wall, whose height was doubled in the same random pattern. A beautiful multi-colored stone that existed as paths on the property was reused in the stairway and step that wraps the courtyard.

Stone even carries some of our memories into this home as samples from other projects are hand set into the colored concrete counters of the kitchen. Ancient stone carvings carrying memories of their history are mounted into the building at key focal points to catch one's eye and celebrate the past, here with us now.

13   View of ceiling in stairway
14   Stair to upper roof terrace
15   Master bathroom vanity
16   Stair to main roof terrace
Opposite:
    Guest room

18   *Detail of seat at master shower*
19   *Detail at master bath vanity*
20   *Detail in guest shower*
21   *Detail of tile and glass beads at table*
Opposite:
      Detail at master bedroom cabinet

18

19

20

21

24

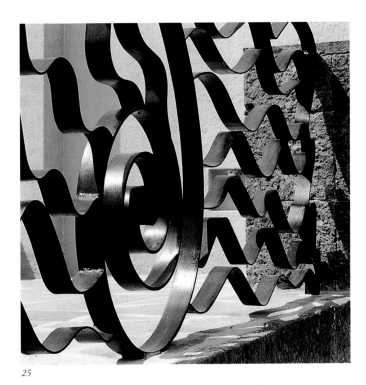

25

26

27

HAMMONDS
RESIDENCE

Oakland, California, USA
Design/Completion 1994/1997

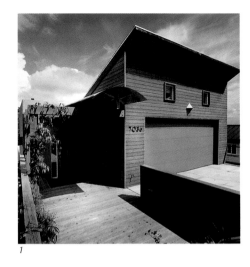

1

2

3

In 1991 a tragic fire in the Oakland hills east of the San Francisco Bay destroyed 2,500 homes, including our client's. The home they lost was typical of California suburban homes built in the canyons in the 1960s. Balanced on long posts, it was completely disconnected from the land as the site plunged below it, inaccessible. This narrow lot slopes steeply to the east, with views to a protected hillside and south through a canyon.

This new 2,800-square-foot house is terraced down the site and pulled apart to create maximum useable outdoor space at the living level and connect the lower level to the ground. The result is three intersecting volumes which cascade down the hill, connected by a huge curving deck.

A vaulted steel canopy at the entry starts the procession as it aligns then pulls you down the multi-layered stairway. By holding the building tight to its north setback line and spreading the rooms apart, the main living spaces are surrounded with windows on all sides with varied views and outdoor spaces. The kitchen captures the morning sun while the living room receives both the sunrise and the sunset. The circular dining room spills onto the curving terrace and is flooded with natural light from every side. Guest rooms, tucked under the garage, are oriented to their own private deck. The master suite at the lowest level opens onto a lush, shaded garden as well as a soaring balcony with distant views.

With strong geometry in the forms, we chose a simple palette of wood and stucco, detailed with steel. Maple and cherry are combined in the cabinets to become furniture. Black plaster at the fireplace is troweled smooth above a floating steel plate hearth. A canted steel newel post, deck railings and the dining room trellis are detailed in stainless steel cables. The soft taupes and grays of the exterior stucco and wood are drawn directly from the site.

1   West facade from street
2   North facade
3   View of terrace
Opposite:
    South elevation from below

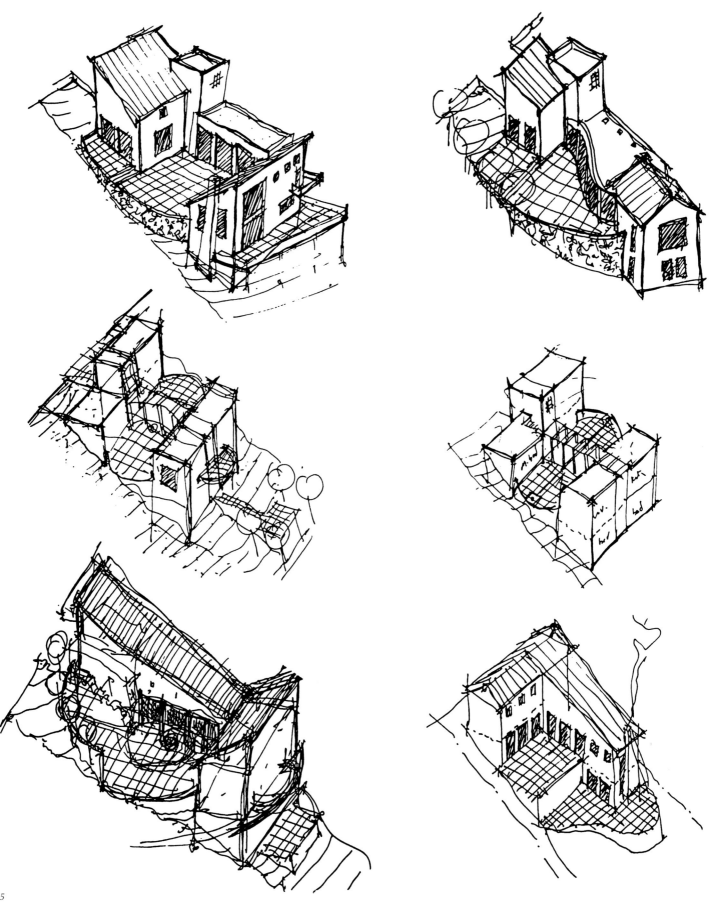

5

5 Design sketches
6 Axonometric, section and details

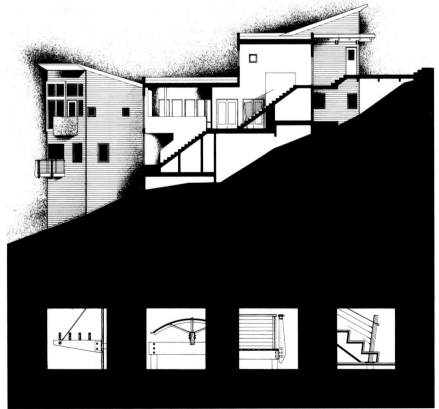

6

8

9

Opposite:
   Kitchen view toward dining room
8   *Dining room with kitchen beyond*
9   *Living room view toward kitchen*

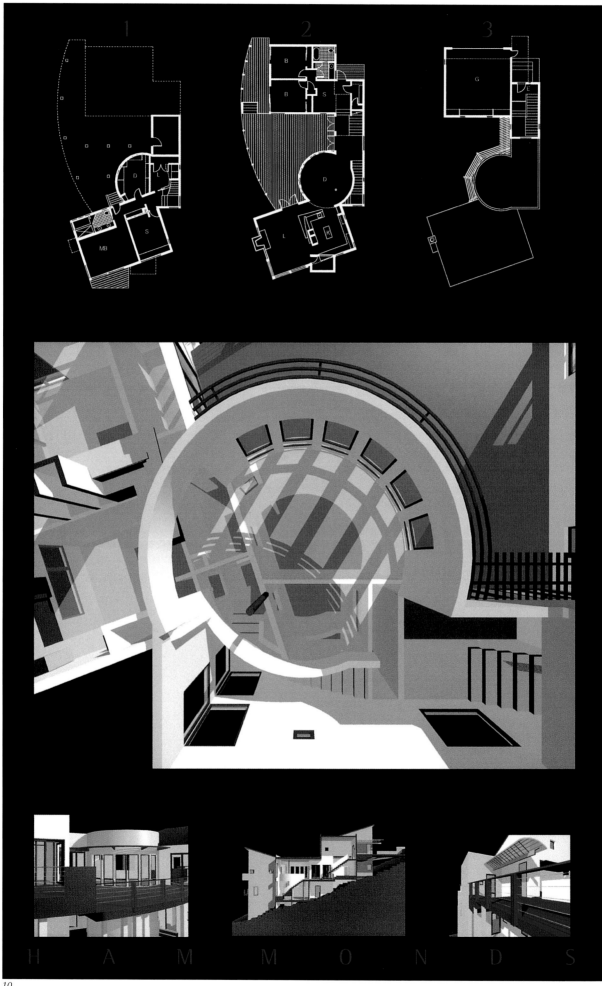

11

12

13

14

SELECTED WORKS

ALTA RESIDENCE
Oakland, California, USA
Design/Completion 1992/1994

This 2,000-square-foot home soars up its site on a steep hillside in the fire-ravaged Oakland hills. Plum colored stucco, teal washed siding and wood shingles combine with the openings to break the mass into highly controlled compositions. Views to San Francisco and the Bay fill windows; the home is intimately tied to the outside at each level. The garage roof creates a large terrace off the living room while the dining room spills into a private patio surrounded by terraced gardens. The bedrooms link directly to the upper garden and a large play yard above.

BLAKE RESIDENCE
Tiburon, California, USA
Design/Completion 1991/1993

This 1950s tract home was stripped, gutted, refaced and expanded to create a new 2,500-square-foot home. The master suite at the upper level straddles the entry, creating soaring two-story spaces split by a connecting bridge. Clerestory windows flood the space with light. Purpleheart wood inlays, exposed wood trusses, layers of trims, sand-blasted glass, copper roofing, and patinaed railings add texture and color, materials and details, reminiscent of the craftsman period, with contemporary overtones.

TOBIN CLARK RESIDENCE
Hillsborough, California, USA
Design/Completion 1988/1990

An 80-foot-long by 25-foot-high skylit gallery pulls in positive energies at the eastern entry of this 8,000-square-foot home built within the guidelines of traditional Chinese feng shui. Crystal quartz inlaid in the floor design is lit from below and aligns intersecting axes with the solstice and equinox. Pure geometric forms intermingle with eastern philosophies to create a contemporary home of classic proportions.

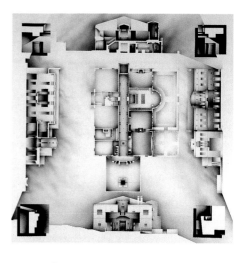

squares @ the east facade

squares @ north elevation

golden rectangles @ the east facade

golden rectangles @ north elevation

rail @ entry

rail @ balcony

organization of squares

organization golden rectangles

NELSON RESIDENCE

Philo, California, USA
Design/Completion 1996/1999

Two hours north of San Francisco in the California wine country, this 60-foot by 60-foot home with an interior garden and deep-set porches on two sides is a tranquil Zen-like form in an untamed landscape. Corrugated, galvanized steel siding and roofing reflects the sky and trees, changing color throughout the day. Broad expanses of composed windows puncture the walls and frame the views. Concrete floors, maple cabinetry and zinc and stone counters complete a simple palette.

PHOTOTIME LABORATORY

Palo Alto, California, USA
Design/Completion 1991/1993

This facility provides state-of-the-art film processing, computer graphics and high-tech portraiture. A rotated square defined in the carpet sets critical alignments for lighting, furniture and walls. A tall, curving wall sheathed in riveted, brushed stainless steel is sliced open to emit a magenta glow, reflected in the polished steel beyond. Maple and steel furniture complement the neon signage and burnished steel railings. A large column concealing existing ductwork is hand-colored in layers of purple and green plaster.

WOOD RESIDENCE

Hillsborough, California, USA
Design/Completion 1996/1998

This home presents a solid facade to the street but all the rooms open through walls of glass onto private decks and gardens toward views at the rear. Tight vertical wood siding and sand-floated stucco, with crisp details in wood and steel, create a clean form set in a lush garden. The three-car-garage is separated from the home, connected with a breezeway and choreographed walk across a fountain and a stone wall. The custom entry door in maple, cherry and ebony is flanked by sand-blasted glass.

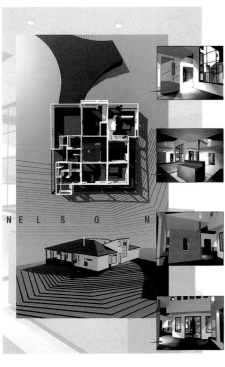

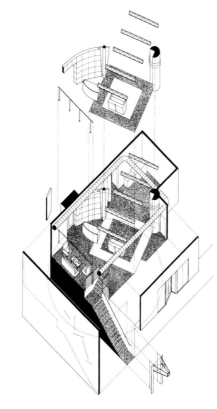

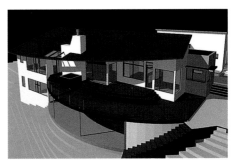

HOUSE 2 FOR 2
San Miguel de Allende, Mexico
Design/Completion 1997/1999

In the heart of Mexico's Central Highlands
at the center of historic San Miguel de Allende,
this home wraps around an ancient pomegranate
tree which shades its central courtyard. With
rooms pulled apart to create multiple gardens,
sunlight pours into every space. An arc of round
columns defines the master bedroom, a line
of square columns defines the dining area. Grids
of windows pull the outside inside, creating a
sense of long vistas and layering of space.

GLANZ RESIDENCE
San Francisco, California, USA
Design/Completion 1994/1996

This 600-square-foot, one-bedroom
condominium with sweeping views from the top
of Russian Hill was gutted and reconfigured with
a gentle geometry of angled and curving forms
integrated into a palette of soft, warm materials.
Long walls of sculpted maple and cherry cabinets
fill a multitude of functions. Subtly colored
concrete and wood counters complement the
stainless steel and sand-blasted glass. The light
wood flooring recalls the California grasses,
providing a warm, clean backdrop for life in
a tiny place.

SIRIUS OFFICE-GALLERY
San Francisco, California, USA
Design/Completion 1990/1991

In San Francisco's warehouse/loft district, this
500-square-foot office/gallery showcases not only
artists, but the artistry of those who created its
various pieces. A local steel artisan forged and
formed the reception desk and curving partition
and tinted them with purple, orange and red oil
paints. A curving, canted wall slices through the
space, hand-troweled in purple, red and ochre
plaster.

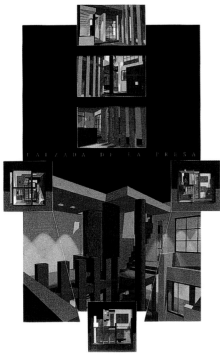

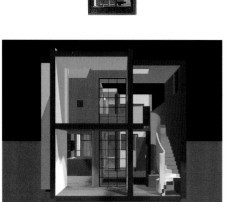

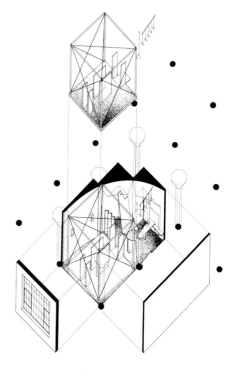

VESTRICH RESIDENCE
San Francisco, California, USA
Design/Completion 1997/1998

Perched on top of Telegraph Hill, this 1,300-square-foot condominium was reshaped with sculpted and punctured walls and a luscious palette of materials and color. Deep reds against silver leaf, shades of taupe and gray, yellows shading to gold—the walls are hand-glazed in multiple layers. The entry was defined with a round coffer, glowing with red fluting and fiber optic lighting glinting on a silver leaf ceiling and columns.

GREENWOOD BEACH RESIDENCE
Tiburon, California, USA
Design/Completion 1989/1991

In a waterfront community north of San Francisco, little bungalows, originally built as weekend retreats, line the shore. Adding a 3,000-square-foot home in the midst of these demanded specific attention to scale and proportion. Each room expresses itself as an independent piece and they cascade down the site like a village cluster. Cedar siding and shingles further differentiate the components. Carefully composed geometric window patterns and a soft, translucent stain tie the pieces into a whole.

SURI RESIDENCE
Tarzana, California, USA
Design/Completion 1990/–

In the Los Angeles suburb of Tarzana, this 14,500-square-foot home alludes to the owner's Middle Eastern ancestry. Stylized sphinxes flank the broad entry steps over the offset curved reflecting pool. The rigid formal symmetry demanded a pair of stairways but is countered by industrial steel columns and a private discotheque. The vaulted family room roof is disengaged at its side walls to float above the space below. Inlays of semiprecious stone details in the entry hall floor tell the story of the home's design.

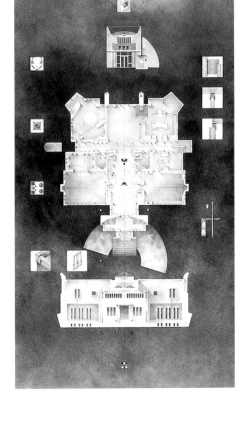

ABBOTT-ELPERS RESIDENCE
Woodside, California, USA
Design/Completion 1986/1988

A downsloping, wooded site was the starting point for a retreat from busy work lives for two mental health professionals. Sun diagrams, view angles and intense analysis of personal needs led to a simple plan. Living, dining, kitchen and master bedroom open onto a broad western deck overlooking the Pacific Ocean. Secondary rooms face into a protected eastern courtyard bounded by the detached garage and guest room. A band of clerestory windows pulls in the morning sun and deep eaves frame the sunset. For the ultimate escape, the study loft soars above it all.

CHALK HILL ESTATE
Healdsburg, California, USA
Design/Completion 1991/–

In northern California's wine country a contemporary Roman Villa is designed to crown a double knoll overlooking the vineyards. A long processional through the gardens opens to a grand entry and large central courtyard. Views from the living room sweep the landscape while the master suite sits above like a crystal cylinder in a rhythm of rough hewn log columns. Skewed to align with a distant peak, the columned temple form of the dining room anchors one corner with the tower/library at the other.

LORD RESIDENCE
Belmont, California, USA
Design/Completion 1997/1999

A landscape contractor and an artist each respond to different qualities of their site south of San Francisco. He is drawn to the distant views and the Bay beyond, she to the treetops and the forested canyon. Intersecting wings in this 2,400-square-foot home provide distinct opportunities for each room to interact with the land. The vaulted roof forms bend under the tree canopies and reflect the sloping hillside. Colors are drawn from nature—green and golden stuccos, natural woods, olive slate, black granite, steel troweled plaster and a green and aubergine carpet that mimics the forest floor.

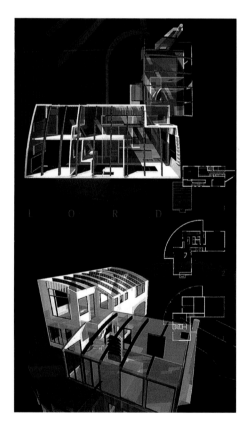

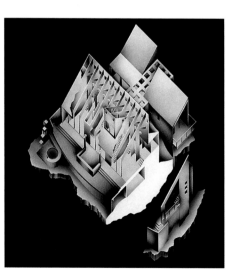

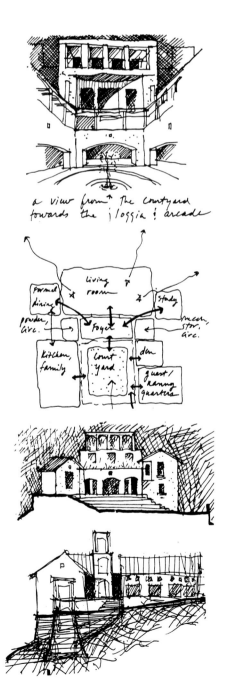

FOXGLOVE FLOWER SHOP

San Francisco, California, USA
Design/Completion 1986/1987

In this downtown San Francisco flower shop the budget demanded the simplest of detail. Display cases for flowers, cards and baskets, as well as a small fountain and utility storage are built from high density board. All surfaces are sprayed with multi-gray shaded paint, leaving adequate funds for lighting, a bold neon sign and a beautiful tiled floor. The neutral palette never conflicts, acting as a stage backdrop for the merchandise.

BUSH STREET CONDOMINIUMS

San Francisco, California, USA
Design/Completion 1987/1990

In San Francisco's Western Addition a Redevelopment Agency regulation allowed a reinterpretation of the standard 40% rear yard setback. Two condominium units at the front, two at the back and two along the east side allowed the garden space to be centrally located, shared and easily accessed by each unit. The facade echoes the bay windows and wood siding typical along this street, without replicating the historic forms.

MONTGOMERY STREET RESIDENCE

San Francisco, California, USA
Design/Completion 1995/1997

Two units were combined for the owner of a multi unit building on San Francisco's Telegraph Hill. His private elevator adds detail to an otherwise plain facade. Inside, sweeping views to the Bay and its bridges compete with the details of anigree and stainless steel, limestone and jade marble. The custom bar sink sits free of the stone counters on either side, a focal point for fun and formal entertaining.

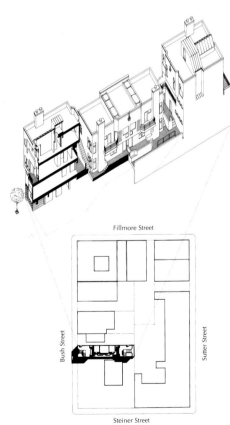

Fillmore Street

Bush Street

Sutter Street

Steiner Street

SCHREY RESIDENCE

Roatan, Honduras
Design/Completion 1994/1996

On the eastern shore of Parrot Tree Plantation, a private resort on the Caribbean island of Roatan, this home embraces more than just the beach. An entry courtyard steps up from the front garden in layers, bound by the living room, guest rooms and garage. The master suite opens onto its own private garden. The living, dining and kitchen areas open onto a multi-layered terrace which spills through a lush garden that opens onto the tropical paradise of a white sand beach.

ZANEY-MORGAN RESIDENCE

San Francisco, California, USA
Design/Completion 1990/1992

In San Francisco's Noe Valley district the tree lined streets are graced with a beautiful collection of Victorian homes. The front rooms were in good condition but the laundry and rear facade was stripped away, the kitchen was gutted and a new kitchen, and family room with master suite above added 500 square feet to this urban home. Balconies above and a large terrace below link the spaces to the garden while the stepped and curving forms pull light in from every side.

ROOSEVELT WAY RESIDENCE

San Francisco, California, USA
Design/Completion 1997/–

Dropping 37 feet from the back to the front, this site, high on San Francisco's Twin Peaks, thrusts this home into the air in a tower of interlocking forms. Huge grids of windows puncture long masses of wall to balance vertical and horizontal planes. An interior lap pool is anchored underground at one end and flies high above the street at the other. The zigzag layout gives ample expanse of windows to the narrow facade, assuring views from every space.

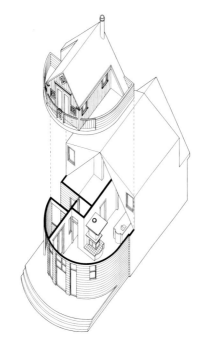

KA HALE KUKUNA RESIDENCE
Maui, Hawaii, USA
Design/Completion 1991/1993

To enter this home on the Hawaiian Island of Maui one must walk across a fountain which divides the house into two wings. A two-story wooden screen, lush with tropical vines, embraces a very private garden that protects the bedroom wing from the street. The cubic form of the bath/changing room engages the thick curving, canted wall of the living room. A complex array of windows and cabinetry in this wall contrasts the garden facade of glass which can be folded away to open the living areas to the pool and gardens beyond.

REINER RESIDENCE
Mill Valley, California, USA
Design/Completion 1990/1992

A family room at the lower floor with children's bedrooms above, provide a surprising new face to the rear of a simple suburban ranch style home. Horizontal wood siding complements the original home's board and batten, and the curve under a simple gabled roof creates shadows that change throughout the day. Lavender stucco boxes define porches and baths and connect the new to the old. The interior was reworked and colored in a palette to showcase the owner's art.

RAFTER RESIDENCE
Los Altos, California, USA
Design/Completion 1995/1997

In this garage-become-playroom, phase one of a whole house remodel, cabinets are the key to order and creativity. A long drawing table with an endless roll of paper tops a set of mobile carts, each carrying a different set of toys. A wall of sliding panels display art projects and swing out to form a framed theater setting—ready for the latest show. The leggo table tucks under this multi-doored storage unit that houses books and games.

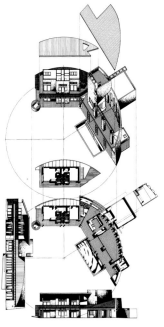

Photography: William Helsel

Steven and Cathi House and their associates endeavor to create beauty, serenity and awe in their work. Their greatest inspiration comes from the subtleties of each site and the deepest recesses of their clients' souls. Through intimate analysis, they mold each project into a unique, magical and harmonious environment. They strive to lift themselves and their clients to a higher level of perception of the world through skillful manipulation of form, light and texture. The poetic quality of their work derives from the simpler side of life: the magic sparkle of sunlight raking across a textured wall, the drama of surprise in turning a corner, the luminous glow of color at the moment of twilight...

In 1970 Steven and Cathi met as students at the College of Architecture at Virginia Tech. Married four years later, they worked in Philadelphia until 1976 when they took a year to travel and study in Europe. In 1977 they moved to San Francisco and worked in various architectural firms until 1981. They spent another year in Europe developing studies of vernacular architecture and on their return created an exhibition entitled 'Mediterranean Indigenous Architecture - timeless solutions for the human habitat', a critical analysis of village architecture in Greece, Italy, Yugoslavia and Spain.

Steven and Cathi began their firm, House + House, in San Francisco in 1982. They have produced a diverse body of work that demonstrates their passion for site specific, well choreographed buildings throughout the San Francisco Bay area, the Sierra Nevada Mountains, Florida, Hawaii, Mexico, and the Caribbean.

In 1989 *Architecture* magazine selected House + House from over 600 entries to feature in their "Discovery" issue on emerging talent. Since then, House + House has received more than 30 design awards and has been featured in numerous national and international publications. Steven and Cathi House have lectured at universities around the United States and both serve on the Advisory Council for the College of Architecture and Urban Studies at Virginia Tech.

PARTNERS
Steven House, AIA
Cathi House

ARCHITECTURAL
Michael Baushke
Shawn Brown
James Cathcart
Mark English
David Haun
Richard Kent
Luis Mercado
Sonya N.Sotinsky
Andre Straja
Michael Tauber
David Thompson
Doug Thompson
John Thompson
Marilyn Thompson
Bess Wiersema

ADMINISTRATIVE
Marilyn Atkinson
Caroline Cooper
Robert Coven
Jennie Ginna
Anita Gordon
Shana Ireland
Mimi Malayan
Michelle Price

INTERNS
Annette Aust
Nilus de Matran
Jin Ah Park
Daniel Pitera
Kyle Prenslow
Teresa Ross

SELECTED BIBLIOGRAPHY

AIA. *The American House - Design for Living* (The AIA Press, and The Images Publishing Group Pty Ltd, 1992) pp. 24—27.

Anderson, Grace. 'On a Windy Hill', *Architectural Record*, May 1990, p. 27.

Balint, Juliana. 'L'Essenzialita Moltiplica Gli Spazi', *Brava Casa*, September 1995, pp. 180–187.

Balint, Juliana. 'Privacy Boven Intimiteit', *Eigenhuis & Interieur*, June 1992, pp. 52–57.

Balint, Juliana. 'Skulptur-Huset Er Bygget Til Moblerne', *BoBedre*, N.r. 8. 1992, pp. 40–45.

Bertelson, Ann. 'The Geometry of Light', *Northern California Home & Garden*, June 1991, Cover & pp. 58–67.

Biagi, Marco. 'Modello al Vero', *Ville Giardini*, June 1997, Cover & pp. 10–17.

Bocchino, Rafaella. 'Rifare la Corte', *Ville Giardini*, April 1998, pp. 18–25.

Bradford, Susan. 'House for Two Architects', *Builder*, October 1996, Cover & pp. 21, 65–66, 68–71.

Bradford, Susan. 'Ruins to Riches', *San Francisco Examiner*, November 24, 1996, pp. E1–E3.

Cohan, Tony. Levick, Melba. Takahashi, Masako. *Mexicolor* (Chronicle Books 1998) pp. 124–125.

Dickenson, Duo. *Expressive Details* (McGraw-Hill 1996) pp. 116–121, 172–173, 212–215.

Edwards, Alexandra. *Fireplaces* (Chronicle Books 1992) pp. 44–45.

Freeman, Allen. 'Entertaining Spaces', *Architecture*, October 1989, pp. 74–75.

Higgins, Lisa. 'Casa Not Blanca', *Metropolitan Home*, January/February 1997, pp. 78–81.

'Home Again', *San Francisco Examiner*, November 21, 1993, pp. F1–F7.

House, Cathi & Steven. 'Economical by Design', *Fine Homebuilding*, May 1994, pp. 54–57.

House, Cathi & Steven. 'Home in the Hills', *Fine Homebuilding*, Spring 1993, pp. 78–81.

House, Cathi & Steven. 'A Courtyard House in Old Mexico', *Fine Homebuilding*, Spring 1999.

Laseau, Paul. *Architectural Drawing - Options for Design* (Design Press 1991). pp. 35, 74, 75, 84, 115, 183.

Lloyd, Peter. *San Francisco - A Guide to Recent Architecture* (Ellipsis London Limited-Konemann 1997) pp. 266–267, 274–275.

Lloyd, Peter. *San Francisco Houses After the Fire* (Ellipsis London Limited-Konemann 1977) p. 16.

Lobdell, Heather. 'A Fresh Start', *Home & Garden*, Winter, 1995, pp. 49–57.

Margolies, Jane. 'The American Dream: Can you (or your children) Afford It', *House Beautiful*, February 1992, p. 79.

McCloud, Kevin. *Lighting Style* (Simon & Schuster 1995) p. 87.

Miller, Charles. 'A Contemporary Farmhouse', *Fine Homebuilding*, September 1993, pp. 82–87.

Mizrahil, Monique. 'Geometrie Naturali', *Brava Casa*, October 1996, pp. 188–193.

Novitski, B.J. 'Digital Architects', *Architectural Record*, February 1999.

Pilaroscia, Jill. *Colors for Living Kitchens* (Rockport Publishers Inc., 1995) pp. 38, 47, 86.

Pittel, Christine. *Great Style* (Hearst Books 1996) p. 146.

Ritter, Joachim. 'Phototime Office Laboratory & Sirius Gallery', *DBZ*, October 1994, pp. 46–49, 50–53.

Ritter, Joachim. 'Whonhauserweiterung in Hillsborough', *DBZ*, May 1993, pp. 34–39.

Roverselli, Elena. 'Dinamismo E Luminosita', *La Mia Casa*, March 1996, pp. 52–57.

Ryder, Lee. 'When Prices Bar Building a House, Remodel', *The New York Times*, October 24, 1991, pp. C1–C6.

Saeks, Diane Dorrans. 'House Equals More than an Addition', *San Francisco Examiner*, July 24, 1991, pp. 1 & 2.

Saeks, Diane Dorrans. 'Up From the Ashes', *Residential Architect*, July/August 1998, pp. 82–87.

Saeks, Diane Dorrans. 'Rising Above it All', *The San Jose Mercury News* - West Magazine, April 12, 1989, pp. 24–25.

Starr, Kevin. 'A House With a History', *San Francisco Examiner* Image Magazine, February 26, 1989, pp. 27–29.

Sutro, Dirk. *West Coast Wave - New California Houses* (Van Nostrand Reinhold 1994) pp. 27–31.

Trelstad, Julie M. *Country Houses* (The Taunton Press Inc. 1996) pp. 60–65, 118–121.

Trucco, Terry. *Color Details and Design* (PBC International 1998) pp. 50–53, 92–95, 128–129.

Uddin, M. Saleh. *Axonometric and Oblique Drawing* (McGraw-Hill 1997) pp. 85, 90, 112, 125, 166, 167, 182, 183, 201.

Warfield, James P. 'Mediterranean Indigenous Architecture Revisited', Reflections - *Journal of the School of Architecture, University of Illinois*, Fall 1985, pp. 50–59.

Whitely, Peter O. 'Bringing in Daylight...With a Hall', *Sunset*, January 1992, pp. 80–81.

Whitmarsh, Linda. 'Cutting Edge Kitchen', *Home*, October 1993, pp. 126–129.

Yee, Rendow. *Architectural Drawing* (John Wiley & Sons, Inc. 1997) Cover & pp. 94, 113, 131, 164, 167, 175, 352, 542–544, 546–549, 587, 606.

ABBOTT-ELPERS RESIDENCE

Project Team: Steven House, Cathi House, Doug Thompson, David Thompson, Mark English
Structural: SOHA
Contractor: Covert & Associates
Landscape Architect: William Peters
Rendering: Mark English
Photographer: Gerald Ratto

ALTA RESIDENCE

Project Team: Steven House, Cathi House, David Thompson
Structural: Dominic Chu
Contractor: Peterson-Mullin
Photographer: Mark Johnson

BLAKE RESIDENCE

Project Team: Steven House, Cathi House, David Thompson, Mark English
Structural: Dominic Chu
Contractor: Paul White Construction
Photographer: Gerald Ratto
Awards: Remodeling Design Award–Project of the Year, Renaissance Design Award

BUCKINGHAM WAY RESIDENCE

Project Team: Steven House, Cathi House, Michael Baushke, David Thompson
Structural: Dominic Chu
Contractor: Covert & Associates
Rendering: Michael Baushke
Photographers: Claudio Santini (3–5, 7, 8, 10); Norman Plate (1, 9)
Awards: Remodeling Design Award, Builder's Choice Design Award, Renaissance Design Award, ASID Design Excellence Award

BUSH STREET CONDOMINIUMS

Project Team: Steven House, Cathi House, Doug Thompson, David Thompson
Structural: Dominic Chu
Contractor: Walsh & Sons
Rendering: Michael Baushke
Photographer: Gerald Ratto

CHALK HILL ESTATE

Project Team: Cathi House, Steven House, Mark English, Richard Kent, David Haun
Structural: Dominic Chu
Lighting: Luminella
Rendering: Mark English

FOREST VIEW RESIDENCE

Project Team: Cathi House, Steven House, David Thompson, Mark English
Structural: Dominic Chu
Contractor: Fulwiler/James
Lighting: Luminella
Landscape: Delaney & Cochran Inc.
Renderings: Mark English (9, 10); David Thompson (5)
Photographers: Courtesy of *House Beautiful*, © July 1992, The Hearst Corporation, All Rights Reserved. Christopher Irion, photographer (1–14, 18); Alan Weintraub (15–17)
Awards: ASID Grand Award, Renaissance Design Award, Diffa Design Achievement Award, Remodeling Design Award

FOXGLOVE FLOWER SHOP

Project Team: Steven House, Cathi House, David Thompson
Contractor: Ken Schuster
Photographer: Gerald Ratto

GLANZ RESIDENCE

Project Team: Steven House, Cathi House, Michael Baushke
Contractor: Innovation Builders
Lighting: Luminella
Photographer: Claudio Santini

GRANDVIEW ESTATE

Project Team: Cathi House, Steven House, Michael Baushke, Mark English, David Haun
Structural: Dominic Chu
Contractor: Paul White Construction
Landscape: Lawrence Fleury
Interiors: Osburn Design
Rendering: Shawn Brown
Photographer: Steven House
Award: Custom Home Design Award

GREENWOOD BEACH RESIDENCE

Project Team: Cathi House, Steven House, Mark English
Structural: Dominic Chu
Contractors: Creative Contracting, Innovation Builders
Rendering: Mark English
Photographer: Claudio Santini
Award: Renaissance Design Award

HAMMONDS RESIDENCE

Project Team: Steven House, Cathi House, David Thompson, Michael Baushke
Structural: Dominic Chu
Contractor: Innovation Builders
Interiors: Brukoff Design Associates
Renderings: David Thompson (5); Michael Baushke (6); Shawn Brown (10)
Photographers: Claudio Santini (1, 3, 5–14); Steven House (2, 4)

THE HOMESTEAD

Project Team: Cathi House, David Haun
Structural: Dominic Chu
Contractor: Covert & Associates
Lighting: Luminella
Renderings: Michael Baushke (6); David Haun (7)
Photographers: Courtesy of *Fine Homebuilding* Chuck Miller (3–5, 9, 10); Steven House (1, 2, 8)

A HOUSE FOR TWO ARCHITECTS

Architect: Cathi House
Structural: Dominic Chu
Contractor: Guadalupe Gonzales
Lighting: Luminella
Photographer: Steven House
Awards: Builders Choice Project of the Year, Metropolitan Home of the Year

HOUSE 2 FOR 2

Architect: Cathi House
Structural: Dominic Chu
Contractor: Guadalupe Gonzales
Rendering: Shawn Brown

JARVIS RESIDENCE

Project Team: Steven House, Cathi House, Michael Baushke
Structural: Dominic Chu
Contractor: Claxton Associates
Landscape: Vera Gates
Lighting: Luminella
Photographers: Claudio Santini (7–10); Steven House (1, 2, 6)

KA HALE KUKUNA RESIDENCE

Project Team: Steven House, Cathi House, David Thompson, David Haun
Structural: Dominic Chu
Contractor: Hartley Construction
Lighting: Luminella
Rendering: David Haun
Photographer: Michael French

LANGMAID RESIDENCE

Project Team: Steven House, Cathi House, David Thompson

Structural: Dominic Chu

Contractor: Fulwiler/James

Interiors: Osburn Design

Landscape: William Peters

Rendering: David Haun

Photographers: Mark Darly/ESTO (2, 4, 5, 13–15, 17, 19, 20); David Livingston (10, 16, 18); Claudio Santini (6–9)

Awards: ASID Design Excellence, AIA East Bay Award, Builder's Choice Design Award

LORD RESIDENCE

Project Team: Steven House, Cathi House, David Thompson

Structural: Dominic Chu

Contractor: Innovation Builders

Rendering: Shawn Brown

MONTGOMERY STREET RESIDENCE

Project Team: Steven House, Cathi House, David Haun

Structural: Dominic Chu

Contractor: Claxton Associates

Lighting: Luminella

Photographer: Claudio Santini

NELSON RESIDENCE

Project Team: Cathi House, Michael Baushke, Michael Tauber

Structural: Dominic Chu

Contractor: Innovation Builders

Lighting: Luminella

Rendering: Shawn Brown

Photographer: Steven House

PHOTOTIME LABORATORY

Project Team: Steven House, Mark English

Contractor: Fulwiler/James

Lighting: Luminella

Rendering: Mark English

Photographer: Stephen Shepard Jr.

Awards: Renaissance Design Award, ASID Design Excellence Award

PRIVATE RESIDENCE

Project Team: Cathi House, Steven House, James Cathcart

Structural: Geoff Barrett

Contractor: Covert & Mock

Lighting: Luminella

Renderings: James Cathcart (4, 6–8); Mark English (1)

Photographers: Gerald Ratto (2, 3, 5, 9–12); Steven House (14–17); Phil Harvey (13)

Awards: Gold Nugget Grand Award, AIA Housing Award, Diffa Design Achievement Award

RAFTER RESIDENCE

Project Team: Cathi House, Michael Baushke, Sonya N. Sotinsky

Structural: Dominic Chu

Contractor: Innovation Builders

Photographer: James Carrier

REINER RESIDENCE

Project Team: Steven House, Cathi House, David Thompson

Structural: Dominic Chu

Contractor: Creative Contracting

Photographer: Steven House

ROOSEVELT WAY RESIDENCE

Project Team: Cathi House, Sonya N. Sotinsky

Structural: Dominic Chu, SOHA

Rendering: Shawn Brown

SCHREY RESIDENCE

Project Team: Cathi House, Michael Baushke

Structural: Dominic Chu

Contractor: Parrot Tree Plantation

Lanscape: Vera Gates

Photographer: Cathi House

SIRIUS OFFICE-GALLERY

Project Team: Steven House, Mark English

Contractor: Walsh & Sons

Lighting: Luminella

Rendering: Mark English

Photographer: Alan Weintraub

Award: ASID Design Excellence Award

STINE RESIDENCE

Project Team: Steven House, Cathi House, David Thompson

Structural: Dominic Chu

Contractor: Campi Construction Phase I, Paul White Construction Phase II

Rendering: Michael Baushke (2); Steven House (5)

Photographers: Courtesy of *House Beautiful*, © February 1992, The Hearst Corporation, All Rights Reserved. Christopher Irion, photographer (1–6, 10); Gerald Ratto (7–9); Steven House (12–15)

SURI RESIDENCE

Project Team: Cathi House, Steven House, Michael Baushke, Richard Kent

Structural: Dominic Chu

Lighting: Luminella

Rendering: Michael Baushke

TELEGRAPH HILL RESIDENCE

Project Team: Cathi House, Richard Kent

Structural: Dominic Chu

Contractor: Peterson-Mullin

Lighting: Luminella

Rendering: Michael Baushke

Photographer: Alan Geller

Award: Renaissance Design Award

TOBIN CLARK RESIDENCE

Project Team: Cathi House, Steven House, Mark English

Structural: Dominic Chu

Contractor: Mega & D.K.Construction

Lighting: Luminella

Rendering: Mark English

VESTRICH RESIDENCE

Project Team: Steven House, Cathi House, Sonya N. Sotinsky

Structural: Dominic Chu

Contractor: Paul White Construction

Lighting: Luminella

Special Finishes: Touche Design

Photographer: Claudio Santini

WALDHAUER RESIDENCE

Project Team: Cathi House, Steven House, Mark English

Structural: Dominic Chu

Contractor: Covert & Associates

Lighting: Luminella

Rendering: Mark English

Photographer: Alan Weintraub

WOOD RESIDENCE

Project Team: Steven House, Cathi House, David Thompson, Michael Tauber

Structural: Dominic Chu

Contractor: Innovation Builders

Interiors: Brukoff Design Associates

Landscape: Terra Design

Photographer: Steven House

ZANEY-MORGAN RESIDENCE

Project Team: Cathi House, Steven House, Mark English, David Haun

Structural: Dominic Chu

Contractor: Theil & Hayne

Axonometric: Michael Baushke

Photographer: Mark Darley/ESTO

Awards: Remodeling Design Award, Renaissance Design Award

ACKNOWLEDGMENTS

We are well aware that what we do is not an individual accomplishment, but a collaborative and an evolutionary one. Our families, teachers, colleagues and friends have touched our lives in countless ways that have affected our work. Through their faith in our vision, their patience and perseverance, our clients have given us opportunities to build into reality the body of work included in this monograph. We would like to thank our professors Olivio & Lucy Ferrari, Tom Regan, Gene Egger, Harold Hill, and Ellen Braaten, for the questions they taught us to ask. We are indebted to the countless unknown architects and builders whose work has touched our souls in the course of our travels and forever changed the way we see and think, and to those like Bernard Rudofsky who helped us understand how to integrate our experiences into our work. We are also grateful to each of the great architects throughout history whose buildings have inspired and influenced us.

Over the 16 years we have had this office, many talented young architects have trusted their training into our hands and have devoted themselves wholeheartedly into our projects, constantly challenging us to reach for new levels of understanding and excellence. We would like to acknowledge David Thompson, Mark English, Michael Baushke, Sonya N. Sotinsky, David Haun, James Cathcart, Doug Thompson, Richard Kent and Bess Wiersema for the thought and care they contributed into each of the projects they worked on. We appreciate the excellent builders in whose hands the dreams become reality, the expertise that our consultants bring to the process, and the new visions revealed to us by the photographers who have interpreted and recorded our finished projects. We would like to give special thanks to Marc and Diana Goldstein, Alec Arany and Charles Steger for their support and thoughtful criticism.

We also realize that it is through the dedicated work of publishers and writers focused on architecture that our work is shared and appreciated by more than those few who actually participate in its creation. We are grateful to Tony Cohan for his thoughtful and poetic Introduction. We want to offer special thanks to Paul Latham and Alessina Brooks and their staff at The Images Publishing Group Pty Ltd for their excitement in sharing our work over the years and for publishing this monograph.

Finally, we would particularly like to thank each other for the years of joy we have shared together through a rich and fulfilling collaboration in the discovery of architecture.